TEENS HAPPEN

TEENS HAPPEN

A PARENT'S GUIDE to DECIPHERING
the MOST SECRETIVE of CREATURES

(Written by a teen)

SHEA ROUDA

LIVE OAK
BOOK COMPANY

Published by Live Oak Book Company
Austin, TX
www.liveoakbookcompany.com

Copyright ©2011 Shea Rouda

All rights reserved.

No part of this book may be reproduced, stored in a retrieval system, or transmitted by any means, electronic, mechanical, photocopying, recording, or otherwise, without written permission from the copyright holder.

Distributed by Live Oak Book Company

For ordering information or special discounts for bulk purchases, please contact Live Oak Book Company at PO Box 91869, Austin, TX 78709, 512.891.6100.

Design and composition by Greenleaf Book Group LLC
Cover design by Greenleaf Book Group LLC

Publisher's Cataloging-In-Publication Data
(Prepared by The Donohue Group, Inc.)
Rouda, Shea.
  Teens happen : a parent's guide to deciphering the most secretive of creatures / Shea Rouda. — 1st ed.
    p. ; cm.
"Written by a teen."
ISBN: 978-1-936909-06-3
  1. Parent and teenager—United States. 2. Parenting—United States. 3. Teenagers—Family relationships—United States. 4. Teenagers' writings, American. I. Title.
HQ799.15 .R68 2011
649.12/5   2011932063

Print ISBN: 978-1-936909-06-3
eBook ISBN: 978-1-936909-07-0

First Edition

Contents

Acknowledgments. .vii

Introduction 1

1. Family 3

2. Siblings. 7

3. School 11

4. New Friends. .15

5. Friends Continued (General) 19

6. Sports. 23

7. Privacy 27

8. Dating 31

9. Sex 35

10. Drugs. 39

11. Alcohol 45

12. Driving 51

13. Jobs 55

14. College 61

15. Bullying .65

16. Acne 69

17. Media Influence 73

18. Nutrition and Fitness 77

19. Hygiene! 81

20. Parties 85

21. "Different" Kids 91

22. Curfew 95

23. Social Networking 99

24. Personal Expression 103

Conclusion 105

About the Author 106

Acknowledgments

Thanks to family, friends, and all those who read more than the first page.

Introduction

What you are about to read is history in the making. I am attempting to give you insight on a topic so confusing and so incredible some parents can't even handle it. I'm talking about teenagers. (Imagine sudden and dramatic music in your head, and the previous sentence becomes even scarier!) But why should you trust me and take my advice? After all, I could be someone who knows nothing of this topic; I might even hate kids; or I might just be a volunteer day care worker. But the truth is I love kids. Full disclosure: I am one. That's right, what you just read is no joke. I am a teenager writing a book about teenagers. Ironic, huh?

Here's a little background information so you and I can get to know each other a little better. In the sweltering summer of 1994 a beautiful baby boy was born; his name was Shea Rouda. (What can I say? I'm a modest man.) I spent my first fourteen years growing up in a suburban house in Columbus, Ohio, with my parents, two brothers, and one sister. I spent days outside with friends and nights indoors with family. My summers were spent at a camp in Maine, and I spent the rest of the year in school.

Then, in late 2009, I discovered we were moving to Los Angeles, California. Two weeks after my parents told me, we were gone. I was torn. I didn't speak, didn't look, didn't cry, and didn't want anything but to move back. The only thing I did was eat and sleep (really the only things a teenager needs). I had gone from king of the school, big ol' scary eighth grader, to that new puny freshman kid from Ohio. Not a good transition.

At the beginning of football season I made my first friend, who nicknamed me Corn. It caught on. The whole school referred to me as a vegetable, which obviously did not help my self-esteem or my mood. But eventually I made friends again and came to love the new school and the experience I was having. Life was back to being awesome. That brings us up to date. Almost. When I wrote this book, I was 15 years old, had blond hair and blue eyes and I was almost five-foot-eight. Keep in mind that the views I've captured here reflect my younger self—and some of today's wisdom. Today I am 17 years old; I have the same blond hair and blue eyes; and I'm six-foot-three. But enough about me, let's begin the discovery.

This book has information on everything a parent should know about teenagers. Hopefully it will answer any questions you have about them, whether it involves friends, family, school, drugs, sex, parties, bullies, or any other problems. Without further ado, I introduce chapter 1.

Family

You know what they say—"family first"—so family is the first chapter. This will be the toughest area for me to address because I do not know about your family and what your life is like. What I can hopefully do, though, is speak for your teen. By doing so, I will tell you the most important thing all of us teenagers want: respect.

Just like Aretha Franklin said, we've "got to have a little R-E-S-P-E-C-T." Teenagers want respect and want to be treated like adults, yet still be loved like a child. It's a tough time for parents and kids, but it is the most essential time. I know you might be wondering what happened to your sweet little child and why your little darling suddenly has acne everywhere and is moody. Simply put, it's hormones, and what parents need to learn most is how to ignore it, and, if possible, avoid talking about it unless the child brings it up. This is a very sore topic for most kids and will create an awkward moment. Any negative comment you make about your teen's mood, acne, or behavior will just make it worse. Definitely avoid saying, "Hey, you're starting to get acne!" That's a common mistake; don't let it happen to you! But all of that information plus more will be covered later. For now, let's get back to respect.

Giving your kids respect will make them feel more loved and mature, something all teenagers want, not to mention that respect strengthens the bond between you and your kid for the rest of your lives. Think of adolescence as a test for both of you. Although some will fail, if you make the right choices and handle situations right, the reward for passing will far outweigh the problems you previously encountered.

The second point about family is knowledge and experience. Every child and parent are entwined by a bond, whether it is weak or strong. But the key to a successful relationship and bond is the times you spend together and the ways you connect. The more you know about each other, the better. However, don't mistake this as a license to invade your teenager's privacy, which might be the single worst thing you could do. Believe me, it will cause more problems. If you really want to secretly know about your children and their friends, I suggest a carpool. That is a great time to tune in to the details they exchange. When I say get to know each other, I mean play basketball together or go shopping (advice from my sister), or help your son or daughter with homework or be there to give advice. You need to find a common interest and exploit it. What better way to do this than a family dinner? Whether they are at home or in a restaurant, family dinners are the best times to share information about your day and the problems that came up. Try to end the dinner on a good note, though, because it sets the mood for the rest of the night. I suggest doing this every night around a dinner table, *not* a TV. But occasionally ordering pizza on a Friday night and getting the gang together for a movie, especially if it's a comedy, never hurts anything.

Now let's look at some tips from an outside source: the one and only Kaira Rouda, a.k.a. my mom!

Question: What is the best thing a family can do to strengthen bonds and connections?

Answer: To create a strong family, you must make traditions and establish a culture. The best way to do this is on vacations, holidays, and special occasions, but day-to-day connections are the most important. This means little things, like sticking up for one another, saying please and thank you, laughing together, or simply chewing with your mouth closed (that's my family's pet peeve; it's our own little cultural rule). These everyday habits will create your family's traditions and keep your home life fun and safe.

In conclusion, family basics are the foundation for strengthening your connection with your teen.

Siblings

Siblings are the most continuously changing factor for most teenagers, next to friends, but then again brothers and sisters are practically the best friends your child may have. You could consider siblings to be like a group of friends. I know from firsthand experience that there are a lot of variables for siblings. Earlier this year I was best friends with my older brother; however, when he went to college I started spending more time with my older sister and became better friends with her. Now my younger brother, older sister, and I have an equal friendship, with my older brother not too far behind. A big tip for parents is to recognize the connections their children have with one another, and keep the strong relationships strong and improve the weaker bonds. I highly recommend creating time for all of the siblings to be together in fun ways. But if you force us to hang out together, for instance making us drive each other around, that might make us resent one another and not want to be together. Try to find a happy middle, such as going to amusement parks, having get-togethers with family and friends, or taking a vacation.

Previously in this chapter I mentioned "variables for siblings." Some people might be confused about what I mean, so I have developed a *variable-rometer*. This is my extremely creative way of saying there are a range of variables that affect the bonds among a child's siblings.

Variable one: college. This is a big one. Whether a sibling is at college across a city, state, country, or even on a different continent, I can't stress enough that visits are the number-one priority for maintaining relationships among siblings, as well as between you and your child who's away. Also, if possible, include your college student in as many trips as possible, yet allow this sibling to have some holidays away from the family to hang with college friends.

Variable two: age. Obviously, age impacts children greatly. I guarantee that you will not find the same relationship between a sixteen-year-old and a two-year-old as you will between a fifteen-year-old and a seventeen-year-old. Closeness in age is a very important factor when it comes to sibling connections. If you're on the love boat, try to keep the kids close in age because it helps greatly later when the kids enter their teenage years—closer ages allow siblings to connect with one another more. It will be rough during the early years with all the mayhem of diapers and pediatricians, but it'll be beneficial when your kids enter their teen years. For parents who already have kids that are close in age, I applaud you. But if your kids aren't close in age, don't worry. It's always heartwarming to see an older teen taking care of a younger sibling, and if you're a guy like me, taking care of a much younger sibling or relative makes you a chick magnet (yeah, we can use old-school terminology).

Variable three: school. This one sort of applies to age. Basically, being in the same school is always helpful. Your children can wave to each other in the halls, help each other with homework, and connect to each other with friends and teachers. If your kids are really close in age (such as twins) and have the same friends, maybe they can even hang together during school. Being in the same school, either public or private, is awesome and should always be used to the best advantage. Make sure you tell your kid this—you could even say Shea Rouda said so. If they ask "Who's that?", simply say he's a beautiful baby boy born in 1994. Works every time.

Variable four: number of children. Clearly a family with twelve children will have a much harder time establishing sibling connections than a family with two children. But don't throw in the towel yet; there are many great things a large family can do. Basketball, football, board games, and many other group activities are just a few. Small families can do the same kinds of things; however, some extra manpower might be needed, and I suggest getting the neighbors to come over or call up some friends. I have a middle-size family of four kids. We love outdoor activities and board games, but if you're feeling mentally and physically exhausted, just pop in a good ol' movie and fire up the popcorn.

Variable five: gender. This one is a biggie. It's a lot easier for same-sex children to form connections. My brothers and I are almost like a gang, but having girl advice from an older sister, or even a younger sister, is always appreciated. If your family is full of both genders, try to incorporate awesome bonding tools that everybody likes, such as squirt-gun fights, snowball fights, building forts (some teens like me still enjoy this), or even playing video games. Come to think of it, a parent who is good at video games would be incredible—you would practically be considered a god in the eyes of some teenagers—but if you are good at video games, don't play them with your kids excessively, and don't beat them too much, either!

Siblings are the foundation of a successful family, and for parents to think they have no control over sibling bonds is an incorrect assumption. Use the tips I gave you in this chapter, and remember, when you get the gang together, have fun and keep in mind that sibling rivalry is not always a bad thing! (That was cheesy.)

3

School

This is another rough topic, but it's extremely important. I have never had too much trouble with school. I usually score either a 3.9 or 4.0 and take all honors classes, and I'm also writing a book. I guess you could call me an overachiever. But some of my best friends get less than a 2.0. This led me to wonder what causes them to not want to put forth effort or work hard.

After extensive research and interviews I have found the answer: nothing! That's right, nothing motivates them to get such a low grade, and nothing motivates them to get a high grade, either. The key word is *motivate*. If you don't motivate your child to form successful study habits or help with homework when needed, then you're failing the Shea Rouda guide to being a helpful parent. As a teenager I know that encouragement and support are the best things a parent can offer. Trust me, if you encourage your children to do well, you'll be surprised how much better they will do in school and life. As an exaggerated example, if your daughter or son walked in the door from school every day and the first thing you said was, "Hey kiddo, just wanted to let you know that your grades are terrible and you suck!" then clearly your kid would have no motivation for school or anything else. Now from a different standpoint, if your child came home every day to compliments—whether they're about clothes, grades, or individuality—I guarantee your child will feel better and be more motivated to get down to business (i.e., school).

Another way you can help your kids with school is by providing resources. It is more than annoying when you finally bring yourself together to work on a project and *bam!* there are no supplies in sight. Keep a surplus of supplies at your house, like posters, markers, tape, paper, pens, and pencils. Also tell your teenager to let you know if a project is coming up so you can avoid a last-minute scramble for supplies. If you want to be a super parent, you could even help your teen with research and creating the project itself. This is easily one of the most helpful things my parents do. When I have to go that one extra mile, I can always rely on my parents to give me help. However, don't become the do-it-all for your kid. Nobody gains anything from that, only a false grade and a false sense of satisfaction. Then again, don't do so little that you barely help your child in a major time of need. Once again, you need to find the happy middle.

The best thing parents can do is take a load off their child's back by helping with the little things, like making breakfast (make sure it's healthy), packing a lunch, helping with laundry, or helping with homework or extracurricular activities. By doing these simple tasks, you'll greatly reduce your child's daily stress, whether it's from school, friends, family, or even themselves.

Never let your child go to school on a bad note. Always send your kid off with something positive, like "Make it a grrrreat day!" or "I love you!" Make sure you don't embarrass them, though, when you do this. Try to avoid saying things like that in front of a large group of friends, unless it's okay with your child.

Let's look at what happens if you don't send your kids off to school on a good note. They'll go to school angry, they'll be less focused on their work, their friends will either help them feel better or get annoying (typically the latter), and if they're really aggravated, their whole day might even be ruined. Definitely avoid morning fights and arguments; instead, have peaceful conversations or laugh during breakfast.

New Friends

Friends are my area of expertise (I say humbly), for I've made new friends many times. I've been to different camps, schools, states, cities, countries, and have had a job. All of these experiences allowed me to explore and perfect the art of making friends. Let's go into more detail with a *vocabulary-rometer*, which I'll use to describe the best ways to make friends and the things a teenager must do to make friends at a new school.

Phase one: exploration. When I say exploration, I mean your teens need to get to know their surroundings. Your teens should figure out the school, styles, people, personalities, groups (or cliques) and slowly try to blend in; they shouldn't lose their heritage or culture, but they should become more like their surroundings. When your teens do this, people will be more confident in asking them about their past and where they've been. (Completion time of phase one: one to two months.)

Phase two: be nice and easy. Hopefully your teens won't immediately go out and demand attention or try to make a statement, like starting a fight, wearing out-of-the-norm clothing, disrupting class, etc. First impressions are everything in high school; new kids shouldn't be labeled as "that kid." Instead, they should be nice and mellow. They should start conversations and share intriguing facts about themselves to bring up their history, and they should not be afraid to ask questions about other people. I find the best way to start a new conversation with someone you don't know is either to plainly say your name and ask for theirs or to ask a question related to the topic you and your acquaintance are occupied with, such as at practice or school. Your teens should be as approachable as possible and have confidence, but not too much—cocky teenagers are some of the most annoying and disliked people in high school. (Completion time of phase two: one to three months.)

Phase three: go full swing. When your teens have made their first friend, they should start hanging out with him or her. Hopefully your teens do not constantly pester their friend(s) to hang out; that would be a mistake and would portray them as an annoyance. Your teen should treat a new friendship like a first date that went well. Don't call the new friend all the time and obsess over the new relationship. Instead, hang out occasionally, strengthen the friendship, and simultaneously meet new people and become friends with them by using the steps in phase two. After your teens have a secure group of friends, they can start to focus on other things. (Completion time of phase three: two months.)

Phase four: meet the opposite sex. By now people should know your teens. Have them take advantage of this and try to meet some people of another gender. This will boost their self-esteem and get their name around. Make sure they're nice and not too pushy. They should be cool and collected as well. In reality, your teens will most likely make friends with both genders simultaneously. The only reason I bring this up is due to stupid competition between teenagers. If your teen is a guy and he meets a lot of girls quickly, then he will be envied by other guys and probably disliked by them. The same applies to girls. Unfortunately, jealousy flows like a river in high school, and it's best to avoid the current. (Phase four is never-ending; there will always be new people to meet.)

Phase five: keep it up. Your teens now have a secure group of friends with multiple outside sources. Make sure they keep up that swag and continue to be nice and fun. Your teens should always meet new people, and hopefully they are enjoying their experience. A new school isn't always bad. That's something that took me a while to learn. (Completion of all phases: three to seven months for phases one through three; phases four and five are never ending.)

Don't fret if it's taking your child longer to work through the phases. If your child is in middle school, it most likely will take longer. After all, middle school is where the strongest bonds are made and groups of friends are formed. In early high school (and even in later high school), friends are constantly switching around due to the vast numbers of kids; therefore it's slightly easier to make friends there. Still, it's a fun and interesting challenge. Friend-making will take your teen through "peaks and valleys, twists and turns" (gotta love that quote from T.I., and hopefully there's more peaks than valleys). If your teen follows these steps, I'm sure it will go smoothly and allow for easy friend-making opportunities.

Friends Continued (General)

Friends are the greatest thing about school, sports, jobs, and practically everything in the world. Can you imagine what a heartless and boring world it would be if no one knew one another? It would be completely terrible! That's why we have friends—to help us with our problems, cheer us up when we're down, and always be there for one another. But what if your child's problems aren't something a friend can help with? Maybe your child's friend is the one causing the problem. Hopefully I'll be able to solve your teenager's problems, or at least give good advice.

Friends can sometimes be the meanest people alive, especially during fights when they might know too much about you. It's worse for girls. I'm truly very amazed with what some girls go through in middle school and high school due to mean friends or friends who are not understanding. If your teen loses one or two friends, then the relationship is not meant to be, and that's okay. A mean friend is better lost than had. But if your teen is losing multiple friends at a time, the problem could be him or her.

Another thing that changes friendships is conformity. Lack of conformity leads to a lack of friends. We end up flowing in a river-like motion. Let's picture the coolest kid in school as a lake. That one person now influences every single person along the river that flows from the lake, sort of like a chain reaction. If the coolest kid does something, then the next person does it, and so on. The second your teen blocks this flow is the exact second the criticism will start. This is much more apparent in middle school than high school, but it's still there. Unfortunately, if your child is under the waterfall of this river, it will be hard to get out of, but it's still possible. Just like climbing a waterfall, it takes time, and as they say, time heals everything.

If something bad happens, such as an incident with a girlfriend or boyfriend, don't fret! Give your child comforting advice. That always helps, but if your teen wants alone time, be sure to give it. Oh yeah, here's a secret hint: If you ask "What's wrong?" and a teen says "I'm just tired" or "I don't feel that well, that's all," about half the time the teen is lying and focusing on something that's troubling him or her. If you want to test the "I don't feel well" remark, then I suggest saying, "Would you like me to get you some Advil or Tylenol?" If the teen says no, then spark a question. If the answer is yes, than grab the medicine and conclude the teen actually isn't feeling well. For the "tired" statement, it's okay to ask what's on the teen's mind, but if the answer is "Nothing, it doesn't matter," then leave it at that for now. Maybe bring it up again later.

Don't be immediately alarmed by the behavior of the kids your teen hangs out with. It's possible that they're just nervous around another parent, or maybe they're shy, so don't jump to conclusions. But if they always act odd or guilty around you, then you have a right to be suspicious. A great tool for figuring things out about your child's friends is to ask another one of your children about the friend. If you have only one kid, ask other parents about kids in the neighborhood and what they've heard. Yet again, a carpool is a mischievous tool that works. Basically I'm saying don't judge a book by its cover (funny to hear that while reading a book). I know it may sound clichéd, but it's very true—kids express themselves in many ways, more than ever nowadays, so just because they dress oddly or act different, it doesn't mean they actually are a bad influence.

However, if you have that gut feeling about a certain friend, or that the kid wearing the leather jacket, driving the Mustang, and smoking a cigarette might actually not be so good after all, you're probably right, and I suggest talking to your kid about it. If your kid is really intent on not talking about it or becomes moody and defensive, I recommend apologizing, then letting it be. Don't continue on a bad subject, *ever*.

The last topic is short but very important. Do not live off of your teenager's popularity! If your kid is a hit at school, don't act like you're the popular one by throwing parties for your kid's friends, allowing drinking, or giving up all of your adult standards to cope with irresponsible actions. Don't act like a teenager and forget your responsible adult senses. If you do act like this, your child will never have a role model. But don't go overboard in the opposite direction and become that uptight and strict parent, either. Give your child free time and independence, and I guarantee you'll be rewarded with respect, admiration, and love.

Friends can be the greatest thing or the worst thing to ever hit your teen. They can become worst enemies or best friends; it just depends on how your child handles life. Try not to let your teenager overreact to small things or be constantly mean or super cocky. All of these things will hurt your child's reputation and give him or her a bad name. Instead, try to teach your kid to act openly and treat all friends fairly. If a problem arises with your teenager and a friend, don't contact the parents of the other child unless it's an absolute must. Talk your teen through the situation and provide a shoulder to lean on and a sympathetic ear. Love is the key to any problem.

6

Sports

When the pressures of school and other things life may dish out become too overwhelming, there's always one place where kids can retreat to and be themselves, where they can blow off steam and work to their fullest physical potential. I am of course talking about sports, and if your child doesn't play any, I highly recommend that he or she pick one up. After all, there are so many out there! (By the way, other extra-curricular activities are great, too. My siblings are very involved in the performing and visual arts. But I still think sports—getting endorphins flowing—is imporant.) But what if your teenager is more of an independent worker than a team player? There are many awesome sports for independent people, such as golf, tennis, skiing, track, gymnastics, weight lifting, wrestling, motorcycling, fencing, and so on. Here are three major reasons your child should at least consider playing a sport.

One: health. Everyone knows that nothing can be more healthy than living a physically active life, and what better way to do this than play a sport? Not to mention, if you enroll your kids in sports when they're young, by the time they reach their early teens they'll already have the building blocks to living a healthy life. I know this worked for me. When I was little I played basketball, soccer, football, and lacrosse, and I skied. I tried surfing when we went on vacations, too (didn't work out so well). In high school, I play basketball and football, and I am very thankful that my parents signed me up for sports sooner rather than later. Experience is key in sports (but remember, it's better to start playing late than to never play at all). Had it not been for my early practices and enrollment in sports, I don't know where I'd be now. Sports have helped me keep fit and stay healthy, not to mention that they relieve the everyday pressures I have as a teenager. I'm sure they will do the same for your child.

Two: friends. Every sport has a close-knit community of players who look out for one another and lend a hand to those in need. With the vast number of students playing sports, this community is growing larger than ever before, so why not have your kid be a part of it? After all, nothing is better than having sports friends that your teenager can always rely on. In most cases these friends will overlap with school friends. This allows for existing bonds to become stronger and opens doors to meeting new people. It's a win-win situation!

Three: opportunities. Sports have so many opportunities—it's unbelievable. Your child will be recognized by parents, friends, colleges, and organizations. They allow kids to stand out from the crowd and find out who they are. Sports are always a good path to take on the road to self-discovery—something all teens go through. Not only will people notice your child and provide compliments, but the school will, too. Let's say your teen has managed to hold above a 3.5 GPA and still plays a sport. Well, now your child has a college resume perk: he or she is a scholar athlete, and this is a big deal. All colleges look for this accomplishment because it represents your child's capabilities, work ethic, and responsibility. This is pretty much the cherry on top of the cake, which sort of makes me hungry. Oh yeah, that reminds me. With all of the calories your kids will be burning, they will be able to eat whatever they want, and that, my friend, is a glorious achievement.

Ultimately, sports are the best way to relieve stresses or problems and help your child become a more successful and mature young adult. Sports teach an area of self-discipline that can't be taught anywhere else. This discipline is fundamental to the development of respect and good behavior. Nothing will whip a teenager into mental and physical shape faster than a sport, and with all the positive attributes of sports, why not give it a go?

Privacy

Privacy is one of the major problems you'll run into with your child, simply because we teens think we want independence, but we don't know how to go about getting it (very confusing, I know). So in reaction to that, we seclude ourselves. This may lead to mistrust or curiosity about what we're doing, but it's secretly just our form of relaxation. Granted, some teenagers engage in other acts rather than just relaxing, but I won't go into detail because those acts are rather obvious. But think about it: if we teenagers were constantly in the eye of parents, teachers, and other kids, we would have people running our lives for us. So we form our own peaceful times when we can get control of ourselves, relax, and contemplate our day. Without this small form of independence, kids would go crazy. Here's another tip: small gestures that say "Please leave" are actually commands, though they are commonly mistaken for requests. Never stall too long if your teenager wants you gone—that's a no-no. Unless your child is being punished, then it's clearly okay to leave him or her alone. Here are three reasons why you should give your teen privacy.

One: relaxation. Of course, we all need our relaxation, and as I said, we teens find that the best way to relax is to be alone. So please do not disturb us. When we are in our state of relaxation, nothing pisses us off more than a call saying, "Honey! You need to do your homework!" or "Did you do all of your chores?" This is something that will make teens resent you. However, chores are necessary, so I advocate for having a specific chore day, such as Sunday. This permits your child to get in a routine and plan relaxation times appropriately and in a manner that does not interfere with chores or homework. Another tip is that once we get crackin' on our homework, whatever you do, *don't stop us*. Some teenagers find it extremely hard to pick up again from where they left off. This causes their minds to drift and focus on other things, such as Facebook, e-mail, or just surfing the Internet.

Two: escape the world. When we teenagers are alone we're able to forget about all the stresses in life and focus on other things, or maybe just take a nap. Then, as soon as we're disturbed, we snap right back into busy human mode and remember all the stresses and problems. Here's some quick advice: allow your child to relax a little bit and muster up some strength before sitting down and getting to work on a major project. It's sort of like working out on an empty stomach. Sure, you might feel good after you finish the workout, but soon the wave of tiredness will hit you, and all of a sudden you're on the floor collapsed and weak. Again, when we're escaping from the world, please don't bother us.

Three: talk to friends. When we teens are alone we like to talk to friends from school on Facebook, Twitter, MySpace, iChat, etc. Contrary to popular belief, we are fine with our parents knowing most of the things we talk about, but at other times we prefer to keep it a secret. As a parent you must recognize that and respect it. This goes all the way back to the respect rule in chapter one. Just as you're entitled to your privacy, teens are too, and when you forget this and cross the boundary, I promise that problems will arise. So to avoid this I highly suggest not putting virtual controls on the Internet or phones after we reach the age of fourteen. By that time kids can figure out almost any way around the barrier. We are very crafty with technology, after all. Instead, if it's absolutely necessary to create limitations, enforce mental rules, not physical ones. For example, have a rule that all kids must be offline by ten o'clock. The teen will still try to find a way around it but will also have a sense of guilt. If we get past a virtual barrier, we just feel accomplished, not guilty.

Getting enough sleep is key, so you definitely don't want to have your teen staying up too late on school nights, or else we're very crabby and depressed throughout the day. To remedy this, either make mental rules about technology or just stop by your teen's room at a designated time to say goodnight and tell them that it's time to get to sleep. Good habits start from a young age, so make sure your kids go to bed early when they're young. It'll pave the way for future habits.

In conclusion, privacy is the utmost thing to understand and respect, and the sooner you do that, the better off you'll be.

Dating

Dating is always a tough thing for a parent to accept. No longer does your sweet little child think "Eww girls/boys have cooties." Hormones have taken over. But obviously I'm not going to argue for why dating is bad. Instead, I'm going to show you why teenage dating is a good thing, and I'm going to do it with another list. However, not all dating is good. For instance, if your teenager is dating someone who's bad influence, then there are reasons to disconnect the relationship. But how can you tell whether someone is a bad influence or not? I'll also provide a list for distinguishing a bad influence from a good influence. Let's start with why dating is good.

One: social skills. Your teenager is set for life after overcoming the awkward moments of one-on-one dates. After all, most major tasks in business involve some form of awkward moments, whether it be speeches, interviews, or starting a new job. Simply allowing dating helps your child learn social skills that will carry through to future years in the workforce.

Two: manners and respect. When kids date, they are on their best behavior to try to impress that special someone. We learn respect, maturity, and manners. Nobody likes going on a date with someone who acts rude and immature, especially dates that chew with their mouth open or talk obnoxiously loud. And so by learning this, teens strive to become better with manners and develop improved etiquette.

Three: fun. It is very true that people are friendliest when they're happy. And when could you possibly be more happy than during a successful and fun relationship? So given this, your teenager will be much happier in a relationship. Who doesn't want his or her kid to be happy? The only person I can think of is Cinderella's stepmother, so don't let that be you! Yes, there are times where your child will experience hardships or even get dumped, but that's where you get to step up to the plate and boost your parent–child bonds and earn some brownie points. And if all goes well, your teen will be back on his or her feet in no time.

So now you've decided to let your teenager date, but how can the new girlfriend or boyfriend be trusted? To help with this I've developed a brand-new tool called the modern-day date helper-outer. Consider it a sidekick during those everyday moments when you judge your teenager's boyfriend or girlfriend.

One: manners. Are they appropriate? If the girlfriend or boyfriend dresses nicely, cleans themselves up, and gives you respect, then typically they've been raised well. A well-raised kid will be courteous and gentle to your child, and that's a positive.

Two: spunk. A date with a lively personality is always good for your child. Usually people like this are nice and fun to be around. That's exactly what you want. However, if the date isn't spunky, it could just be shyness or nervousness. This is no problem, but a little character never hurts anything.

Three: decision making. What I mean by decision making is what your teenager's date chooses to do. For example, if dates want to take your child to go out to eat or to a movie, that means they're good-hearted. However, if they think going to a Mickey D's or Wendy's is the right thing to do, then they're sadly mistaken. Look for these things when judging the girlfriend or boyfriend.

Now you know how to spot a bad influence and a good influence, thanks to your new modern-day helper-outer. So after all of this, why not let your child date? It will benefit your child and provide a better understanding of how the world works. And if you feel that the date is a bad influence, you have the power to terminate the relationship or influence your child away from that person. Go for it.

9

Sex

The chapter most of you have been waiting for is finally here. Brace yourself, because things are about to get crazy. First of all, did you know that a study conducted by the Guttmacher Institute (www.guttmacher.org) discovered that by age nineteen, seven out of ten teenagers have had sex? Now that may not seem surprising, but listen to this: a study by the same group found that of the 18.9 million new cases of sexually-transmitted diseases (STDs) each year, 9.1 million (48 percent) of them occur among fifteen- to twenty-four-year-olds, and although that age group represents only one-quarter of the sexually active population, they account for nearly half of all new STDs each year! Wow, now that's a shocker. But before you go and give your teens "the talk" and tell them to be abstinent, consider this: we know.

Yes, we already know. We have constant talks about being abstinent—during school, during meals, at home, everywhere! We understand the risks of sex and are fully aware of the outcomes it can create. With this in mind, it doesn't mean you should completely ignore this topic, but you should minimize it. Nothing creates a more tense and awkward moment than a talk about sex, especially if the talk is mom to son or dad to daughter. But enough about recommendations; it's time to learn about today's teenagers.

In recent observations I have discovered that the majority of teenagers have their first sexual intercourse (I feel nerdy saying that) in their junior or senior year. Sex is very rare in middle school and slightly less uncommon in freshman year. Sophomore year captures about 15 to 20 percent of the population, then junior year comes and everything changes. By senior year, I'd say about 75 to 85 percent of teenagers have had sex. This doesn't apply for "half sex," though (oral and other stuff). For oral, I'd say freshman year captures about 15 percent of the students, then there's a steady increase to 85 percent by senior year.

Having been in a big school and a small school, I have noted that lower grades in smaller schools have a more sexually active student body than big schools. However, big schools catch up by senior year, then both school types are relatively similar. This varies, though, depending on the type of school. For instance, I have discussed this with friends from other schools and found that inner-city schools are more sexually active compared to suburban schools. Also, schools with less funding and poor health services typically have a more sexually active student body.

It's pretty obvious, especially in high school, that girls will have sex before guys. Some of you might be wondering why. Here's the simple answer: upperclassmen. They swoop in and steal all of the girls in our grade. And because they're more sexually advanced than freshmen, they influence the younger girls, causing them to follow the same path and become more sexual as well.

Another topic that I need to clarify is teen pregnancy. Through all of the schools I've been to and had connections with, I don't know one girl who has become pregnant. This seems to become more well understood as teen pregnancy rates fall. This could be due to improved use of condoms or birth control pills, or simply because some teens are choosing to wait. In any case, teen pregnancy is becoming less common, and parents need to realize this. With recent attention and media coverage, it seems that most parents think it's a major problem, but truly, it's rare.

I hope you've learned some facts about teenage sex and you'll be able to make the right choices with your teens. They already know about the consequences, but on occasion—well, actually let's change that—a rare reminder about the dangers of sex is acceptable. But don't make your speech public, a mistake my dad made in a restaurant by talking too loud. Instead, keep it private and don't bring it up out of the blue. Make sure it applies to a previous conversation, and when I say previous I mean within an hour, or to a question your teenager brought up about sex. Basically, inform us occasionally, but don't preach.

Drugs

Another chapter you have been waiting for is finally here! First, did you know that the average age of first use of marijuana is fourteen, and for alcohol is twelve (www.aacap.org)? Now that's early, and the starting age for both drugs is quickly getting younger. Why? Because we teenagers think we're immune. We believe that the choices we make today will have no affect on our life tomorrow, and because of that we think we can try what we want, when we want. As a parent it is very important to get across the message that it will cause problems. However, if you become the super-naggy parent who won't let your child do anything or see anything, your kid will rebel.

"Rebel: to oppose or disobey one in authority or control, to act in or show opposition or disobedience" (www.dictionary.com). Don't let that rebel child be yours. After all, it is quite possible that your son or daughter could rebel if you're one of the parents out there who pushes too hard against drugs. When a parent or guardian pushes too hard against drugs and says "You can never do this or that," well, one day your teenager will think, "What if I *do* try this or that?" Then your teenager will be on the road of no easy return. When kids jump on that wagon, everything becomes more alive. They'll begin to try new things (drugs) and experiment more. This results in poor attention and reduced effort in class and is preceded or followed by less respect toward parents and elders. And that's the last thing you want to happen, because now not only do you have a troubled teen, but you also have an unmanageable and dissociative teen. So how do you find the perfect balance?

This is similar to your approach to dating, and I'll refer to this as the balance or the middle. This point of balance occurs when parents occasionally remind their teens of the consequences, but never overwhelm them. In order to create this middle, you must understand that information is the best weapon against teen drug abuse. Tell us stuff we haven't heard in school a thousand times. Get more creative than telling us marijuana is a gateway drug (if I had a nickel for all the times I heard that!). I know the previous sentence might go against what I said earlier about we teens understanding about dating and drugs and that we hear all about it at school and whatnot. But when I say providing information I mostly mean talking about your experiences with drugs and alcohol, because most likely you have had experiences. I always find that some of the best connections and deep conversations between children and adults involve honest conversations about these experiences. They allow a personal connection like no other. I remember the first time I learned my parents had tried drugs. It shocked me. But now it has set an example of what not to do and what to do.

First of all, I learned that if I follow in my dad's footsteps (party hard), then the college I want to go to might close its doors to me and never open them again. On the other hand, if I follow my mom's path (Never party! It will kill you!), then I won't learn from the world and get the full high-school and college experience. I don't mean that all there is to college and high school is partying; I'm saying that by going down either of these paths, your kid won't have a true and fun childhood. That's why I believe my parents got married, to balance out their lives and find a middle. Teenagers ultimately choose whether to stop partying or to continue partying through life, and the only factor that will influence their decision is how their parents raise them.

But now that I have given you an insider's view of drugs and alcohol from the eyes of a teenager, let's look at my personally compiled statistics from talking to friends and teens across the nation.

National Household Survey on Drug Abuse (NHSDA Report) (oad.samhsa.gov):

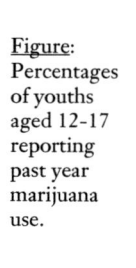

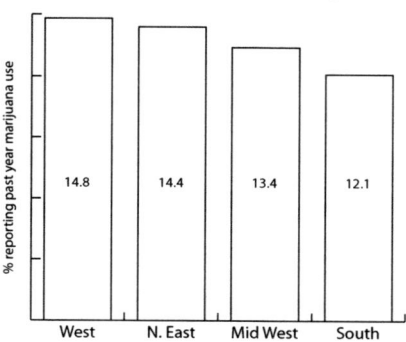

Figure: Percentages of youths aged 12-17 reporting past year marijuana use.

West	N. East	Mid West	South
14.8	14.4	13.4	12.1

(% reporting past year marijuana use)

Big school versus small school: These types of schools have about the same usage; however, if one person starts at a small school, the rest will typically follow because with fewer kids, it's hard to get out of closer and more compact groups of friends.

Boys versus girls: There is really no difference here, except that maybe guys tend to start a month or so sooner than girls. Although guys may start sooner, the effects are much more serious and dangerous for girls due to less body mass.

City versus rural: City teenagers are more frequent users because there are more dealers, more demand, and more influence, and drugs are imported more than in rural areas. However, some people create drug labs or pot farms in rural locations, which in turn greatly affects the local area because they supply the products for cities and towns.

Age: By twelfth grade at least half of the students have tried a drug. If you don't believe me, just look at this statistic: by eighth grade 30.3 percent of all teens have tried drugs, by tenth grade 44.9 percent of all teens have tried drugs, and by twelfth grade 52.8 percent of all teens have tried drugs (www.teendrugabuse.org). An even scarier fact is that at the time of a survey, half of all teens reported that they had used a drug in the past thirty days (www.teendrugabuse.org). Now that's ridiculous, but believable.

It seems as if everything these days has become more acceptable. Whether it is drugs, sex, or attitude, life just isn't the same as it was generations ago. And for that reason, you as a parent must recognize that and go with the flow. Accept that more research has been done and that scientists have discovered that being a pothead is less mentally harmful and less addictive than being an alcoholic, and understand that your kids recognize facts like this and others. You must adapt to an ever-changing world and lifestyle and realize that experimentation is part of normal teenage life.

Alcohol

In the same category as drugs but more important, it's now time to look at another problem that affects teenagers: alcohol. So what is alcohol, exactly? It is any

> "flammable, water-miscible liquid, C_2H_5OH, having an ether-like odor and pungent, burning taste, the intoxicating principle of fermented liquors, produced by yeast fermentation of certain carbohydrates, as grains, molasses, starch, or sugar, or obtained synthetically by hydration of ethylene or as a by-product of certain hydrocarbon syntheses: used chiefly as a solvent in the extraction of specific substances, in beverages, medicines, organic synthesis, lotions, tonics, colognes, rubbing compounds, as an automobile radiator antifreeze, and as a rocket fuel"
> (www.dictionary.com).

I have no idea what that description means, but hopefully you do! I did catch the last part, though, and I bet you didn't know they use alcohol in rocket fuel and antifreeze until just now! I know I didn't. But how does it affect our bodies and, more importantly, a teenager's body? Let's find out.

Alcohol is a depressant, which means it slows down brain activity and alters a person's mind, actions, and motor skills. It creates a dangerous yet seemingly fun state for a teenager. Danger and fun are two of the four main things teenagers crave (the other two, of course, are food and sleep). And as Jamie Foxx and T-Pain said, "blame it on the ah-ah-ah-ah-ah alcohol" (if you don't understand what I'm talking about, it's a song about alcohol called "Blame It"; listen to it). Now teenagers have an excuse for every stupid thing we've ever wanted to do. It goes something like this:

> Random person one: "Hey, you want to go crazy tonight?"
>
> Random person two: "First let's get booze, and then we can just blame it on the alcohol!"
>
> Random person one: "Great, I'm sure there won't be any consequences after!"

That dialogue basically describes the weekend of half of all teenagers. No thought, no care, all consequence. I don't know of one weekend when my friends and I have partied and not one of us has gotten in trouble, or as we youngsters say nowadays, busted, rousted, or f***ed. So how many kids drink? I said earlier that about half of all teenagers use drugs. You could argue that alcohol is a drug, which it is, but it's in a separate category. I'd say at least 80 percent of all students, at a minimum, have tried alcohol twice by the time they're seniors in high school. This applies for all schools, all places, all ethnicities, both genders, and practically every teenage demographic you can think of, excluding super-religious schools and boarding schools (don't send your kid to boarding school just to avoid alcohol, though; it's not always the case that the campus is booze-free!). Typically, a kid who is very alcohol-friendly is usually very drug-friendly, but there are some exceptions.

Now here's a secret insider tip to finding stashes and discovering sneaky ways to transport things (my friends will hate me for this!). One stash place for slightly careful teens is between mattresses or under blankets or pillows in cabinets or drawers. Transportation tools for alcohol are bags, sleeping bags, and purses. But I'm going to stop there. Why? Because it's not fair for teenagers if their parents raid all of their belongings, unless it's an absolutely serious matter. However, if you really want to know possible stash spots, just Google "great stash spots" or "great hiding places," or basically anything that includes "hiding" and "spot." But if you do resort to this, then serious trust issues are evident, or you're just excessively curious.

So now I want you to hold your right hand in the air and repeat: "I, as a responsible parent, will choose not to abuse my insider tips received from a reliable source, but instead use my knowledge to better understand and connect with my teenager and gain a stronger knowledge of my teenager's behaviors to prevent extremely stupid or harmful actions." You may now put down your hand—thank you for participating—and if you didn't do as I asked, don't get mad at me for any problems that may arise.

What does alcohol do to your teen that's so bad? Well, binge drinking causes liver failure, cancer, heart failure and disease, and brain damage, and it affects every single organ in the body (www.ncadi.samhsa.gov). This will cause major problems with your teen, both short-term and long-term.

But that's not the worst part—driving is. Did you know that in 2003, 31 percent of drivers aged fifteen to twenty years who died in traffic accidents had been drinking alcohol (www.ncadi.samhsa.gov)? Most of this is due to parent failure—not failure because parents didn't teach their teen enough, but failure because maybe they taught their teen too much all the time. If parents are excessively pushy and strict about alcohol, when their child chooses to drink and goes overboard, the teenager starts to have a panic attack and thinks, "Oh no! What if I get caught! I can't be driven home, it's too obvious! I have to drive home!" Then the next thing that happens is a car crash and a funeral.

So whatever you do, let your child know you won't be mad. Instead, let your teenager know you're there when needed and that you can always pick up your teenager, whenever, wherever. Then, the day after you pick up your teenager, be sure to say, "I'm not mad, I'm just disappointed." That's the old guilt-tripper, and it always works. It doesn't create a pissed off, I hate everything mood in a teen; it causes a "Wow, I really screwed up" sensation. Don't say you're disappointed too much, though, because that will cause just as many problems as saying, "I'm pissed at you, and you're extremely stupid and worthless." In the end, be there for us and later scold us in a sincere, loving, and teaching manner.

Your home should be a home—a place where your kids know that no matter what, they are safe and can always return.

Ultimately, letting your kid drink is a decision that you will have control over in a short time frame (from when they first learn about alcohol to when they reach eighth grade). How you treat your teenager and the amount of respect you show will completely decide your teen's path. Be dedicated and understanding, and I bet your teenager will return the same love and make good decisions. After all, sixteen- to eighteen-year-olds tend to be less likely to drink in excess when they have a close relationship with their mothers (www.medicinenet.com). Food for thought!

Driving

The most important, frightening, and responsible thing your child will accomplish as a teen (next to college, hopefully)—I'm talking about the thing we all fear and love—is driving. It's a pretty scary thought to consider. After all, driving could be the ticket to injury or even death (sorry if I scared anyone), or it could be a tool that makes life easier and your teenager more responsible.

First of all, did you know that car crashes are the leading cause of death for teenagers? Sixteen-year-olds are in more car crashes than all other ages! I know, it's scaring me too, and I already knew that from school. But what if all of these driving accidents could be prevented? I'm not suggesting that the driving age should be raised to seventeen or eighteen. Instead, I'm here to tell you that you've got the power to change these risky habits.

You can save your teen's life by choosing a safe car. Whatever you do, if you have the ability to buy your teen a car, no sports cars. No matter how much bank (money) you have, and no matter how much your teenager begs, just say no! You'll thank me later because, in case you didn't know, sports cars and giant SUVs are the leading vehicles for teen deaths (www.abcactionnews.com). Although giant SUVs can plow through cars, they also roll over the easiest and carry the most passengers, therefore increasing the risk and number of deaths in one crash. In contrast, small cars are the least likely to roll over, but they are the most likely to be decimated in a car crash. The most suitable vehicle is either a midsize SUV or truck. Also, newer cars are typically safer than old ones. By helping your kid pick out a safe and reliable car, you'll dramatically increase the chances of survival in a crash, but it doesn't stop there. You must parent your teenager through the process of learning to drive as well.

If there's one thing I know about driving, it's how necessary it is for a parent to teach you to drive—not a sibling, but a parent. Siblings are usually close in age, correct? So therefore they're less experienced and more inclined to break the law in various ways, like speeding (the number-one cause of crashes), tailgating, and talking on the phone or texting. If they teach a sibling to drive, they will simply hand off these habits to the new driver. However, when parents teach a teenager to drive, they are a better role model and can give great tips from their experience. Sibling-to-sibling driving is a no-no, but tips from siblings, like how to pass the license test or resist pressure to drive fast, are very useful and much appreciated. If no tips or help with driving skills are given, it could cause your teen to turn out like my sister, who crashed into a bush, tree, and fence going three miles per hour on the way to school. Always give constructive criticism and encouragement; otherwise we feel as if we're terrible drivers (that may be true) and will never become better.

Another key aspect is to not freak out in the car when we have our temporary license. A great example is when my mom is in the car with us. My brother, sister, and I have all had to deal with her screaming and frightening and tense comments about our driving. One thing you must realize is that we will make mistakes—like my sister, again, who drove on the wrong side of the road on a highway with my mom in the car! This could have easily been avoided if both of them had remained calm and taken actions for themselves instead of following the driver in front of them, who had made the same mistake. Basically, stay calm and cool then correct any minor or major problem we make in an understanding voice.

So now we've talked about passing that magical license test and advancing from a permit or temporary license to the real thing. Here's the breakdown after we get our license. After talking with my friends and other licensed drivers, I concluded that girl drivers always seem to be safe and mature. However, most guy drivers to follow this path: for the first two weeks I was the safest and most disciplined driver on the road; I never broke any speed limits or laws. But as I said, that was for only two weeks. After that I became confident and wanted to explore my new driving abilities, so for about three weeks after that I was more speedy and aggressive. Shortly after that I entered a middle stage where I was both aggressive and disciplined on the road for another three weeks, but I mostly leaned toward the aggressive side of driving. After this stage I entered the phase I'm currently in (and probably will be for the rest of my life), which I call the situational stage. Although everyone is different, it seems that after about two months or so of driving, most teens become relaxed and confident at the wheel and drive either crazy or disciplined depending on the situation (hence the name). Essentially, give or take a week or two from my experience, and that will represent your teenage boy with his license. As I said earlier, this sequence of driving patterns doesn't always apply to every boy, and it definitely depends on the car your teen drives (sporty cars encourage wilder driving).

With experience comes wisdom. As a parent it is very key to coach your teen driver in a positive and encouraging manner. And remember, paying for our gas is something you should always do—it will definitely make us safer drivers. Just kidding! Paying for gas doesn't make us safer drivers, but it does make you a very nice parent!

13

Jobs

Chances are your child has had a job, whether age ten or eighteen. The job may have been doing chores around the house, running a lemonade stand, selling newspapers, or working at a local restaurant or store. No matter the case, by the time your children are teenagers they should have some work experience. If they don't, well, chances are your kids are either spoiled or uncooperative. Chores and jobs are an absolutely crucial part of developing responsible and respectful teenagers. So when is the time to start chores? When should a request differ from a command? When should you pay for labor? It's time to wait no longer: the answering machine, Shea Rouda, is here.

To start off, I'll state a simple and well-known fact: kids, especially teenagers, are more likely to do tough labor for money. One less obvious thing is that we teenagers are not dogs; we're humans. You can't pay a teenager over and over again for completing the same chore and then one day think, *I'm sure little Johnny will grow up and do it on his own now, and I won't have to pay him!* That's the attitude a dog has—expecting to get a treat, getting denied, then doing the trick again hoping for a treat this time. Teenagers are smarter than that, and lazier, too. If we don't get a reward, chances are your tough task won't get done. But then again you don't want to become a parent that just hands away money.

A set allowance is perfect for any teenager and is a good incentive for doing chores. You could even use my parents' method for allowance. I used to receive an allowance based on my age. When I was fourteen, I got a $14 allowance per week, usually handed out on Friday, in time for the weekend. For every year you add a dollar to the weekly allowance. The sooner children start getting an allowance, the better, because the sooner we get an allowance the quicker we learn to manage money and finish chores for a specific reason (money).

Now let's say there's a time when a certain chore extends beyond normal work, such as creating a patio with stones, cleaning a dirty fountain, replacing sprinkler heads, or taking down holiday decorations. For special projects like this, I suggest giving separate pay. Depending on the task, it could be $10 to $20. This will give us an actual reason to work and not make us mad at you! Isn't that awesome? Looks like money can buy happiness after all.

Here's another tip: encourage us to go to work. When we

decide on a job, like creating a lawn company with friends or working at a local store, automatically say yes and push for it. When teenagers are debating about whether to get a job, parents should help them realize that a job is an awesome idea. First of all, jobs create more money in teenagers' pockets, and if parents help them manage it, they can save up enough for car repairs or any future scenario. Believe me, they will have things to pay for, like broken windows, house damage, and so on. Second, jobs help kids make more friends and connections. It's always good to have connections, especially as a teenager, when life is sometimes at its toughest point. At jobs you can meet responsible figures and learn discipline when you're around your boss. Finally, jobs pave the way for the future. Any experience in the workforce looks good on a resume. Whether it's applying for college or another job, experience is critical.

If your child chooses not to get a job, though, don't be disappointed. That's what I did. I had reasons though, such as keeping up my grades, and I was enrolled in lots of sports. If your teen is on the fence, push for a job, but if your teen decides on no job, respect the decision.

The last topic is requests versus commands. Here's a quick fact that might surprise you: *cognitive limitation* is the proven idea that teenagers don't fully develop the area of the brain attributed to multitasking until late adolescence. This means that although you may command us and ask favors for so many things, we won't be able to do all of them immediately. Yes I know, it's another sudden realization I have just enlightened you with. But in all seriousness, this little fact is very important. You should never overwhelm your teen with chores and tasks. If you do, we stress and freak out, and trust my parents on this one: nothing is worse than an angry, stressed teen.

But now that you've learned to not overload your teen, you must learn when to command and when to ask for favors. Here's the easiest way for me to put it: you should command when the task is necessary and challenging, and ask for a favor when the task is easy and sometimes needed. Here are examples of both:

> **Favor: Hey, could you grab me the newspaper on the street when you go out to play basketball?**
>
> **Command: Clean your room! Don't make me tell you again!**

Both are perfect ways to reach out and get things done when needed. In my experience as a teenager, I have found that you will receive more thanks and get tasks completed much easier when you ask for a favor, not give a command. You might have to ask for the favor more than once, but hey, favors can always turn into commands if you don't get the result you want.

In the end, when you decide to give an allowance and determine the value it has, you must realize that the set amount must fit in with your teenager's life. Don't be afraid to throw in an extra ten bucks if we want to see a movie with friends. It doesn't have to become a regular thing. If it does, though, simply say no and terminate the habit. And always remember to reimburse your teens when we cover costs. For instance, if your family takes a taxi out to dinner and spare cash is needed for a tip but you don't have enough on you, you can ask your teen to cover the tip, but please pay him or her back. Kids shouldn't have to pay for family affairs.

Ultimately, allowances and jobs create better money management habits and develop the work skills we need earlier in life, allowing us to excel in the future.

14

College

"College is the best time of your life. When else are your parents going to spend several thousand dollars a year just for you to go to a strange town and get drunk every night?"

Sorry for that worrisome but truthful quote from David Wood. I just needed to scare you a little bit more before I give you tips about your teen and college. Now I don't have direct experience with this topic, being in high school; however, I listen to my older brother and sister and many friends who are in college, and I read tons of stats from the Internet. Let's address the topic with another statistic. Did you know that 79 percent of all students are accepted by their number-one college (www.moneywatch.com)? But what if they aren't accepted? What if they don't have the grades to go to a college you like? Well, I'm here to help you solve these encounters in a successful manner (I felt like a genius writing that).

Okay, so your teenager hasn't been accepted into the first-choice college. You might be wondering what to do and what to say as horrible thoughts race through your mind. You've noticed by now that your teenager is probably depressed or mad, so steer clear! Talking about it will bring up more thoughts of what could've been or should've been, so definitely avoid it. But at some point you will need to talk about your teen not being accepted. The time for this to happen is immediately after your teen reads the letter (regardless of *any* mood). Say something positive and reassuring about getting into another college or figuring something out. Then later, after your teenager has blown off some steam, it's time for the real talk to begin. Try to limit the reminders of the hoped-for college. For instance, don't say things like "I'm sure Superstrict University wasn't even the right choice for you," or "There are better choices out there than Superstrict University." By avoiding these kinds of comments, you keep the wound from bleeding and can focus on other topics rather than dwelling on the past.

When your conversation has moved on from the rejection, you can begin to talk about the choices. Try to focus on other colleges to apply to, and if you've planned well, there are hopefully other colleges still looking at your teen's application. Basically, with all of the colleges in the world, there will be many places your teenager can go. If you want to look at places with many colleges, consider California, New York, Pennsylvania,

Texas, and Ohio. They have more universities than other states.

Suppose your child was one of the 79 percent of students who were accepted into the first-choice college. Now everyone has to stress with books, tuition, college parties, medical bills, and leaving home. The good news is that 86 percent of kids go to college close to home (www.moneywatch.com). More than likely this includes your child, so that makes leaving home easier, because visits are more convenient. But if your teenager goes to college far away, make sure to have vacations at times that work for everyone, like Thanksgiving or another time when everybody has the same days off.

College parties are a threat to your sweet teenager, for there are drugs and alcohol, *things that I'm sure they've never seen before.* Yeah, that was sarcasm. I guarantee that most of the things that occur during college parties have happened during high school. So don't be afraid of what happens at college parties. Your teen will be able to handle it. I'm sure you remember college parties and all of their craziness, so you can provide tips to help your teen navigate the treacherous waters.

Another thing to deal with are siblings and college. When my brother went to college, he left right when we moved to my new school, so not only did I lose my best friend at the time (my brother), I practically lost all of my friends. It was a rough time, but if there's anything I learned, it's how to deal with this situation. First of all, stay in touch. Always make sure your kids are socializing with one another and visiting. Facebook and cell phones are great for connecting, but what's even better are vacations. After many weeks away and talking only through cyberspace, seeing one another in person is great. It allows your kids to catch up on old times and talk about new experiences. For instance, my brother gives me tips about parties and what college is like, and I tell him what the family is up to and give him inside information on what our parents talk about, such as his broken arm from trying to beat a friend in a boxing match. It's great for the whole family and helps us connect better.

    College will be a tough time and a great experience for everyone in the family. It will strengthen connections and provide a new insight to life for your teen, plus your other children will learn from their sibling's college life and possible mistakes.

15

Bullying

Time for your knuckle sandwich, twerp! Sorry, I had to say that. It immediately came to mind when I thought of bullying. But in all seriousness, bullying is either something your child is a part of as a victim or a villain. Being a victim is the worst. If kids are a target for bullying, they're constantly teased, looked at oddly, and sometimes physically abused (but unlike what Hollywood and your local rumors say, physical bullying does not happen very often, except for those who live in dangerous areas or gang-infested places).

Let's say Jimmy is the king of the school, or maybe Sally is the queen of the school. Suppose Jimmy or Sally gets in a verbal fight with your child. Now Jimmy or Sally hates your child and starts rumors or otherwise manipulates others to hate your child, too. Everyone is affected as the rumors spread down the school hierarchy. Then finally, when the rumors reach everyone in school, your child has become a target for bullying by the whole school. It's tough as hell to break free. I know a couple of kids who are targets, and everyone bullies them, including the opposite gender and sometimes kids from other grades. It's terrible. People can be best friends with a person one day, then the next day they hate that person because of someone else's fight. It's stupid. But if this does happen to your child, don't worry. Just be nice and lay low. Time will heal everything, and eventually things will be okay.

But being the villain can be just as bad. Typically bullies have more inner and outer problems, causing them to raise hell on others to bring themselves up, or else they're simply going with the flow. If your child is a bully, you can stop it, but first you need to recognize it. So how do you tell if your child is a bully? It'll be hard, but the best way to find out is at school-sponsored events and through information from other parents. Frequent trips to the principal's office are obvious signs. Next, you must counteract the bullying. Have a long talk about the bullying with your child. At first you should be mad, actually furious, then be sympathetic and ask why your child is doing it, and remember to play the disappointment card (it always works). Don't do anything drastic at first, like taking away things or a long grounding, unless it was a serious first offense. If it was a minor offense and you dish out unreasonable punishment, your child will be pissed off and think it was the target's fault and go back to bullying even more. Remember that a happy teen will spread happiness, a depressed teen will spread depression, and most importantly, a violent teen will spread violence.

When teenagers are victims of bullying due to the way they look or act, it will eventually subside. Whether the remedy is growing up, making more friends, counteracting the rumors, allowing time to heal problems, or enduring something unexpected from life, their problems will end. And make sure you tell them that. It's okay if it takes time—everything does. Maybe in high school your teenager is a nerd; that's how my brother was freshman and sophomore year. But by the time he was a senior he owned the school. Now he's in college as a freshman, and yet again, he owns the school. It's weird because he was bullied intensely in middle school, but now he's a king. I guess anything is possible. And when teenagers are bullies, it can be fixed. Cure their problems and show them happiness, and I promise they'll show their happiness to their schoolmates.

Ultimately, bullying can be the reason your child becomes depressed and sad in life, but more than likely, it will be motivation to do well and succeed. If this is the case, expect a promising future.

Acne

Whether the face of your child looks as smooth as a newly polished automobile or as spotty as a pepperoni pizza, chances are you've been wondering when acne will start or, in most cases, end. In order to directly answer that question, I used information from a friendly site called About.com, which says that acne typically begins between the ages of ten and thirteen and affects nearly 100 percent of teenagers, including all races, ethnicities, and both genders. At first, acne will start on the nose and, depending on diet and genetics, will either slowly or speedily spread to the forehead, chin, and cheeks. However, some major cases of acne can include the shoulders, back, neck, and upper arms. It usually ends in a person's twenties, but some cases may end earlier or extend longer.

It's important for you to understand how teens view acne. Just think back to when you had it. We all hate it, but we all get it.

Kids often lose focus of that. Sometimes we feel as if one pimple will cause the world of school and friends to hate us or look at us funny, but almost 40 percent of the school will show up that exact same day with a pimple on their face too, so no need to fret. If your teen does have a serious problem with acne, there are many botanicals and creams that can easily reduce or eliminate the problems. If that fails, a simple doctor visit can do wonders as well.

Another thing I would like to address is prevention and care. Preventing acne starts with food; after all, you are what you eat. To have happy skin you have to eat healthy food that is low in bad fats (trans-fatty acid) and sugars, and you have to avoid glycemic carbs. Some foods and drinks that are linked to acne are pork, nuts, excess milk and sugar, cookies, chips, margarine, chocolate, processed foods, and anything containing ingredients with shortening or hydrogenated oil (www.health911.com).

Here's a fun fact: if something says it has zero trans fat per serving but the ingredients say "partially hydrogenated vegetable oil" or "partially hydrogenated soybean oil" or anything hydrogenated, it has trans fat in it. Now you may be wondering how this is possible if the nutrition label says "zero trans fat" or if that's stated on the front of the package. It's because food manufacturers are allowed to round trans fats down to zero. If there are 0.4 grams of trans fat per serving, the company is legally allowed to say the product has *zero* trans fat per serving. Crazy, huh? If the label says zero trans fat, I want them to mean it and not try to sneak something by me. Not cool.

Now you know what causes acne, but what stops it? Not surprisingly, and you hear this for most everything, diet and exercise alone can be a perfectly suitable way to prevent and eventually stop acne altogether. Cardio and any activities that generate a lot of sweat are great for skin because they flush out the pores. Just remember to wash off the dirty sweat, or it can be absorbed back into the skin. However, without water you can't adequately sweat, which is why if you want stellar skin, you must drink lots of water. The recommended amount is eight glasses per day. Water helps to flush out the skin and remove wastes from tissue. Without water, your skin cannot retain its natural shape. It wrinkles easier and becomes saturated with oils.

To achieve incredible skin, an epidermis-friendly diet is necessary. Foods that aid skin health and protection are high in omega-3 (salmon, sardines, walnuts); beta-carotene (carrots, peppers, sweet potatoes, red grapefruit); monounsaturated fats (naturally occurring in olives, avocados, peanut butter, and almonds); isoflavone (beans, alfalfa); polyphenol (grapes, blueberries); and water (watermelon, peaches, celery) (yahoo.com).

The last step in acne prevention occurs when the culprit is already there. Oh yes, it's time for the face-off with the pimple. Let me paint a picture here: It's 7:00 a.m. You're a six-foot, blond-haired, blue-eyed male. You just awoke from your nightly slumber and begin to crawl out of bed to the sound of a horrendous alarm clock screeching like the building is about to self-destruct. Your room has a subtle glow of blue as the morning light squeezes through the dark blue curtains. You limp your way to the bathroom as if you'd done it for twenty years. You turn the lights on. What you see next is bubbly, white, and horrifying. Oh yes, the newest addition to your face, a bulging pimple. Immediately the thought of squeezing it comes to mind; however, you're reluctant, as scars on your face remind you of the marks other pimples left behind. So what do you do? You just have to let it be.

Pimples are your body's way of testing your patience. If you don't pop them, you pass the test and they go away on their own in three days or less (usually). If you give in to the urge to pop that sucker, the outcome seems great at first, but the next week will tell a whole new story. That's right, depending on the size of the pimple, that area where it once was can scar up and last for two days to two weeks—not to mention it's just plain bad for your skin to break it open. So popping pimples is much more negative then letting them run their course.

Ultimately, acne is an unwanted gift from nature, like body odor, and everyone in the world will have it at some point. The sooner teenagers accept this fact, the easier it will be for us to accept our bodies and feel more confident in school. In fact, stressing over acne actually causes more acne. How annoying is that? Basically, let acne run its course, and if it gets bad, apply skin creams or ointments, but avoid taking matters into your hands and, well, using your hands. And always remember the well-known saying: some omega-3, beta-carotene, naturally occurring monounsaturated fats, isoflavone, polyphenol, and water a day keeps the dermatologist away!

Media Influence

Open up a *Playboy* magazine and I guarantee you will see a half-naked woman. No surprise there, right? Go on the American Apparel website and you'll see another half-naked woman (and I literally mean half of her body is naked) selling underwear. Is that inappropriate? The majority of parents will say, "Yes, that is unacceptable! I never knew clothing companies could be so irresponsible! How dare my child shop at that store!" But the reality is (and this may seem crazy) boys and girls are familiar and comfortable with the opposite sex's anatomy. We know what the other gender's reproductive organs are, and most teens are comfortable expressing these thoughts with everyone . . . except their parents. Why? Because we look at parents as teachers and also as friends. When it comes to gossip and other things, parents become like teachers, and we keep our mouths shut. But when it comes to sports, school, activities, help with homework, and anything not involving sex, drugs, and partying, we can tell you a plethora of things.

Sex sells, and companies know that. That's why almost all current textile advertisements aimed at teens show a sexy man or woman, and because we are powerless against our own hormones, we succumb to these pictures and commercials. We strive to be just like the models we see in countless articles and posters, so we buy their clothes. "Why can't I just look like this? Or why can't my face be a little different?" most teenagers say, and those questions all boil down to the clichéd phrase, "No one is perfect." The sooner we accept that, the better off we'll be.

But whatever you do, never tell your kids they are not perfect—that would be stupid. Self-acceptance is something we teenagers must realize over time, and it usually won't occur until we reach our late teens. I find it funny—I'm writing about teens and accepting who we are, but I haven't accepted who I am. It doesn't help that the media portrays how to live a perfect life and how to act and look.

What parents *must* understand is that teenagers are like explorers. At first we have a long journey of emptiness, travelling the unknown of our emotions and life, but eventually we will reach the land of self-discovery and uncover our own path in life. Until then, help make our journey easier. Compliment us on how we look, be vocal on days we look good, and please rarely give us negative comments on days we look bad. I don't mind taking insults from my siblings on how I look, but as soon as one of my parents says I should change this or that, it impacts me a lot more. Understand that you are the one and only greatest influence on your teenager's life. Everything you say and do will have an effect.

If your kid is completely hypnotized by negative media (such as shorts that are too short or shirts that are too big), vocalize your opinions on these matters. For example, if you hate how teenagers sag their pants you could be like my dad and say, "You know in prison, if you sag your pants it suggests to other prisoners that you are willing to be a sex slave." You would not believe the affect this had on my little brother. I swear he has never worn his pants higher. Truly it seems as if using a joking yet serious tone when correcting us on how we wear our clothes is the best way to change our dressing habits, but be sure to use caution when reiterating these opinions, because the more you yell at us, the more pissed off we get.

Parents are one of the largest influences on teenagers. You, as a parent, have more of an effect on your teenagers' opinions than their best friend, especially in middle school and early high school. If you compliment us on days we wear what you want us to wear, and don't compliment us on days we wear something you don't like as much, we will pick up on those hints and choose the clothing you complimented us on. I know it sounds odd, but it's a form of manipulation parents can easily use to secretly influence us to wear what you like, without aggravating us. Trust me, follow these tips and soon enough you'll have more of an impact on your teen's life than MTV could ever hope for.

Nutrition and Fitness

As of 2010, 14 percent of all children aged six to nineteen years were obese. That number is insane, especially because it has nearly tripled in the past twenty years (www.troubledteen101.com).

Many factors can contribute to obesity, such as televisions, the Internet, iPods, comfy couches, and the consumption of factory-made snacks and goodies instead of organic, farm-grown foods. A healthy life starts with a healthy diet (if you are not aware of it, the food pyramid has changed from a vertical orientation with grains at the bottom to a new horizontal format). The best way to keep kids healthy is to give them food with modern sanitation levels but grown with old methods; meaning the food is organic and grown in a farm free of harmful production chemicals and *not* produced in a factory.

However, unless your child is obese (there's a childhood obesity assessment calculator at www.shapeup.org/oap/entry.php), do not control snacks. There's nothing better than coming home from a rough day of school and munching on some cookies or chips, just as long as a banana or a glass of milk goes along with them. That's been my diet my whole life. I figure as long as I'm physically active, an unhealthy snack a day with a healthy food alongside it won't be too much trouble. So far that method has worked perfectly, and I've always maintained a healthy life.

Another tip is to allow your child to snack on mostly what they want, and then when it comes to breakfast, lunch, and dinner, cook what you want them to eat—healthy foods. But once a week an unhealthy meal is always welcomed, such as Taco Tuesday or Pizza Friday, never both in the same week, unless it has been a very active week. Another healthy habit is to pack foods for school lunch and not buy food at school. After all, most schools sell unhealthy pizzas, fatty foods, and nutrition-lacking snacks. There are very few healthy choices, plus most kids spend their lunch money on two cheap pieces of yummy pizza rather than one pretty good sandwich.

Sports are also extremely key to a healthy lifestyle. Not only do they provide exercise and enjoyment, but they also take up the time most kids would spend on a computer and snacking at home. I've found with sports I can't go home and eat unhealthy snacks because by the time I get home from practice it's already dinner time, and I have to eat the healthy meal provided by my parents—bummer! Then after dinner, I'm too full to snack on anything unhealthy. It's a win-win situation. Your healthy dinner is eaten because your kids are starving for anything, and they're not snacking on unhealthy snacks before or shortly after dinner.

Have dinner at a table, not on a couch in front of the TV. Maybe once a month that's okay, but never do that on a daily basis. After all, talking during dinner is one of the best ways to bond and relieve daily stress. Also, limit drinking soda during home dinners; we get enough of it during the rest of the day. I just had to get that off my chest real quick.

One thing my friends and I really enjoy during sport off-seasons is getting a membership at a local gym. If your teenager's school has a gym, most kids can probably work out there for free. Gyms are great because they have trainers that come free with memberships and willingly design a workout that suits teenagers, whether it's cardio or strength training. Also it's a great way to have fun with friends in a healthy and productive manner, not to mention a great stress reliever.

Did you know it's clinically proven that teens who are healthier and exercise more are less stressed with life? And you know the saying that parents are only as happy as their saddest child? I'd like to change that slightly; parents are only as stress-free as their most stressed child. So if your children aren't very stressed, you won't be very stressed, either. And hey, if this chapter were a math problem, then a healthier kid = a less-stressed parent. So remember, healthy food and diet + sports and physical activity = a healthier, happier, and more stress-free child and parent. I should be a mathematician, huh?

Hygiene!

I put an exclamation point next to the word *hygiene* because this is such a funny topic. I remember seventh grade when I would walk down the smelly school hallways and hear all the teachers yell, "Make sure to wear deodorant, kids!" I completely agree with that statement; however, at the time I wasn't aware that I needed to wear deodorant. After all, it's hard to smell your own body odor, and it's even harder when all your life you've never had any body odor and then one day you come to school and everyone plugs their nose when they're around you. This chapter applies more to middle schoolers who are just now discovering the horrifically stinky world of body odor, acne, and grime.

I didn't regularly shower until seventh grade, the same year I discovered I had body odor. It's not so much that kids are against hygiene; it's that they don't understand that they need it. Middle-school teenagers are right at that stage when they get greasy and smelly. In order to help them out (and improve the smell of your house), teach them proper hygiene, such as applying deodorant, showering, brushing their teeth twice a day, and keeping their hands away from their face to avoid acne. If at first they refuse or forget, don't worry—they'll develop these habits soon because kids at school will let them know about how they smell and how dirty they look. As soon as I got a negative remark about how I smelled, I immediately started showering and wearing deodorant. Then when I got my first compliment on my hygiene, I felt more mature and responsible.

But don't overhype hygiene. Teens who wear too much deodorant can cause the exact same reaction as teens who have poor hygiene. Most girls hate being engulfed by a cloud of Axe, and most boys hate being suffocated by a cloud of perfume.

After kids are past their middle school years and go on to high school, chances are they have pretty good hygiene and are relatively problem-free. But what if they aren't? Some funny jokes to alert them about their poor hygiene might snap them into shape, or maybe tell a sibling to go talk to them about showering more or brushing their teeth. If worse comes to worst, you can hide sticks of deodorant or toothpaste in their backpack. That would be funny! But like I said before, never make fun of acne! If your teen stresses over acne, most likely it will only get worse.

Maybe your child is *too* clean and spends five hours in front of the mirror. Well, I guess that's better than being nonhygienic, right? So you can't be too mad. Ways to handle this situation would be to not pay for all the hygiene products or express how natural beauty is much better than covering it up with a ton of makeup. I find that siblings usually do a great job of expressing their parents' feelings toward teenage habits. For instance, one of your kids might say to a sibling, "You spend way too long in front of the mirror!" or "You wear too much makeup!" This is an excellent time to express your point of view and possibly convince your teen that overdoing hygiene can be bad.

Another thing that hinders hygiene is lots of partying. Consumption of alcohol and/or drugs almost always leads to a poor night's sleep. Most likely on party nights when teens sleep out, they will end up spending the night on a dirty couch, floor, or anywhere else that could be grimy. I guarantee they won't brush their teeth or take a shower. So if your child has a problem with being dirty and grimy, partying is not the solution. On the other hand, teenagers have extraordinarily great hygiene before parties and are usually squeaky clean before leaving the house.

In the end, hygiene is a habit teenagers develop for themselves through trial and error. As soon as they find the perfect hygiene ritual, they will stay clean and fresh for a long time.

Parties

From a teenage point of view, nothing is more exciting than hearing that you're invited to a huge party. Honestly, I don't think anything can be more exciting, and if you don't believe me, think back to when you were in high school and college. How awesome was it to hear that a party was scheduled for the weekend? Obviously it was very exciting, and if you disagree, that's only because you're a mature adult now and you try to cover up your party days. Just kidding! But for real, parties are actually one of the best things parents could ask for. Now before you call me crazy, just keep reading.

A party is like an exam or test in the sense that the trust between you and your teen will be tried. If you set rules in your house, such as no drinking until you're twenty-one and no drugs—ever—then a party will be the ultimate test of whether your teen obeys these rules or not. Now some of you may ask,

"That's pretty obvious, Shea, but how will we know if our teen does these things at parties?" Well, you will be able to tell or find out (unless your teen is very, very sneaky, which is difficult).

Parents talk—a lot. Chances are you'll hear about something your teen did at a party from another parent. Whether the information is true is for you to decide. You could even bring it up with your teen. I, for one, love to know what rumors are spread about me through the parent world. But one thing you should know is that the more people the rumor passes through to get to you, the more likely it is to be exaggerated or completely irrelevant. If you're new to the whole cycle of how parents obtain information about teens, here's how it goes: One child tells a parent about what happened at a party and that your child was involved, or parents overhear their kids talking about what your child did at a party. Next, that information may be passed directly to you, or it could be passed on through other parents, but you'll eventually find out. After you hear about it, you should first find out if it's true and *not* jump to conclusions. If it turns out the rumor is true and your child broke your rules, then you have many options.

One: ground your teen. Through all of my research of friends who are always grounded, I found that grounding pretty much does nothing to solve the problem in the long term; it just makes it worse. For real, grounding a teen is a twentieth-century thing. What are you going to do? Force us to stay home for blank amount of time in our rooms where we have cell phones, Internet, TVs, video games, magazines, and tons of other things? All teens do when we get grounded is go to our room, hop on the

Internet (or text some friends), and ventilate about how pissed off we are that we can't be with our friends. Then, after the time has been served, teens might do the exact same thing they got grounded for because it was fun, or they now want to rebel against their parents. So please, be more creative than grounding us after every mistake we make. However, if you hardly ever ground your teen (and I mean like once a year max), then grounding will have an effect on your teen that usually won't cause them to go crazy (as long as the punishment fits the crime.)

Two: increase the chores. Thankfully my parents don't make me do a lot of chores, so this punishment works quite well when I deserve it. Sometimes a little labor is all it takes to bring out the respect in teens. No one likes to do labor, and nobody hates it more than lazy teenagers. So obviously labor and lazy teenagers don't go well together. Maybe breaking the rules involves doing dishes for three or four days, possibly washing the family car, or better yet, washing your car. Who knows what you could do with all these chores? Be creative, but again, make sure the punishment fits the crime.

Three: be more lenient. Really? Yes, really! Don't question the clichéd power of "If respect is given, respect will be received." One thing I admire most about parents is how cool they can be, and an easy way to be cool is to give your teen freedom. That's all we want—freedom! Our whole life we've been told what to do, and sometimes it's nice to be able to make our own choices, and a great time to make choices is at a party. Some people may go nuts when they hear this, but the thing that makes my parents the best in the world is that they trust my choices and let me decide what I do when it comes to partying. Teens who have more trust with their parents are the teens who make better choices and understand the effects of drugs and alcohol. Instead of telling us "Don't do drugs," you need to say to us, "I hope you understand what these drugs will do to you and the effect they will have. It is your choice whether you do them or not; however, if it becomes a problem or interferes with the quality of your life, there will be consequences." *Boom*, not only did you just give your teen freedom, responsibility, the power to make choices, and a life lesson, but you also gave your teen respect, and I guarantee you will get respect back! Talk about killing two birds with one stone, right? Another thing that helps teens make good choices is to vocalize your opinion on certain drugs, but let your teen choose whether or not to do those drugs.

Another tip is to pull out the disappointment card once again. This works much better than the angry card. If you tell your child that you're mad, that conveys a mood, and moods pass. However, if you say you're disappointed, that shows you've lost respect, and teens hate to lose respect. Ultimately, you must ask yourself, "Am I too strict on my teen?" Now pretend you're in the shoes of your teenager and ask, "Are my parents too strict on me?" If you have any reasonable doubt from either point of view that you are too strict, then maybe it's time to loosen up the rules.

Four: take away a privilege. Eh, it's an okay idea, but not always recommended. Sometimes taking away the car or texting for a week will do the trick, but taking away a privilege is just a lesser form of grounding your teen. Unless the crime is an absolutely perfect fit for the punishment, such as no car for a week because you heard your teen was doing donuts in the school parking lot blindfolded, then don't use this punishment very often. Taking away privileges often works best as a threat or warning. For example, you heard your teen was doing doughnuts with the car in the school parking lot. Depending on how nice you're feeling you can either punish your teen or say, "If I hear about this again, you will not have your car for two weeks." This tactic works well on teenagers because we know what to expect if we break the rules, and it gives us an excuse to tell our friends if we want to avoid peer pressure. Here's another good tip on how to punish your teen: you can immediately give us the punishment after we do the crime (such as no driving for a week because your teen misused the car), or you can give a warning and *double* the punishment. Intriguing, right? So now if you hear your teen misused the car, you give a warning and say that if you hear about it again, your teen won't have the car for two weeks. Shaking things up a bit, huh?

Five: other punishment. If you have any other punishment questions, post them to my website (www.TeensHappen.com) and hopefully I'll be able to answer them!

Teenagers today seem to do everything earlier than adults did when they were kids (except for some people in the 1960s). We seem to party a little more, get a little more overserved (intoxicated), and be more wild than our parents ever were. I don't know why teens party more these days. Maybe it's because we have faster and easier ways to have friends over to hang out, maybe it's because we have easier access to alcohol and drugs, or maybe it's just that our generation is wild. Who knows? But whatever it is, parents have to get used to it. You can point out our habits and mistakes, but only we can accept them. So if you think we party too much, tell us. Don't try to force us not to party so much. Just voice your opinion, and sure enough you might see a more responsible teenager.

"Different" Kids

This section applies to those who parent a teenager with mental or physical differences. I'm not going to list any facts about anything relating to special-needs kids because I know as a parent you've already seen and memorized most of them. I'm sure you're worried for your child every day at school and understand the enormous barriers your kid faces. I have the utmost respect for every single parent whom this chapter applies to.

Personally, I am very close to a teen with a form of Autism called Asperger's Syndrome. I watched him get bullied in middle school and I've also watched him grow into a confident, amazing college kid. He was always mainstreamed—and those middle school years were tough. His parents didn't figure out what was up until the bullying had already become a big issue. I don't have a lot of insight on this topic, but I do know it's critical to get involved and stay in the know especially if your teen becomes the victim of bullying and especially if they don't have the social skills to stick up for themselves.

If your teen has been identified for special services, and has an IEP and/or an aid—and he or she is at a public school—I can explain the thoughts and reactions of other kids at school. I can tell you that for the most part teenagers are very sympathetic toward special needs kids. Typically kids talk to and smile at your teenager and give positive reinforcement and authentic expressions. I haven't heard of one case at any of the high schools I've been to where a special needs teen was bullied. However, I am aware that these scenarios occur at some schools. The only reason a teen would ever bully a special needs kid is because they're angry at life and jealous of the love and attention your child receives. It's a shame, but it's true.

Another thing I've noticed is that sometimes special-needs kids can be among the most popular and accepted people at school. I'm thinking of one autistic teen in particular, at my old school, who was about two grades above me who had no fear of asking a girl out. Honestly, he was probably the bravest kid in our entire school. Word spread quickly around the school about who he dated, and there was speculation about who he would make a move on next, until eventually about ten other teens around the school followed in his path. The next thing you knew, relationships in our school skyrocketed about 40 percent, and everyone had respect for the one brave kid who started the whole trend.

At my new high school, there is a teen who happens to be blind and a piano genius. I'm not kidding. He was featured on *60 Minutes*. He's amazing. We are all in awe of his talent.

I'm focusing on the positive, I know, but it's to make a point. Parenting is tough, and if your teen has learning differences or physical limitations, it can be even harder. I know you've learned everything there is to help your teen with what makes him or her different and special. Make sure you also learn about what makes her a regular teenager and remember the bottom line: Respect! (You knew that answer, right?)

Curfew

Easily the most disputed topic in my family, and maybe yours too, is curfew. Without a doubt, it's a very tough fight for both sides. Parents are worried about safety, good choices, and keeping in touch, and teens worry about not having enough time to have fun or be with friends. So how do we solve this problem? Let's find out.

One: reinforce keeping in touch. I know most parents worry about what teenagers are up to, and most of the time they're curious about what our plans are, so what do you do? Text or call us. But if you send more than two texts per hour saying, "What are you doing now?" then you might be pushing it over the limit. On the other hand, never keeping in touch also poses problems. You should establish some sort of pattern, such having your kids text or call every two or three hours to tell you where they are and what they're up to, or have them text or call every time they change locations to more than a block away. Establish some sort of repetition so your kids don't forget.

Two: set an agreeable time. The key word is *agreeable*. Both you and your kids must decide on a time they must be home. This time may change depending on location, time of year, event that is taking place that night, how old your teen is, and the local law enforcement curfew.

Three: enforce the time. Now the most stressful part—enforcement. The best way to enforce a curfew is yelling at us when we're late and saying you're happy to have us home when we're early (in a meaningful, loving voice). Depending on how severely late we are, if we come home at all that night, the punishment might be greater than just yelling at us. If we forget to check in and tell you that we're sleeping out somewhere, then you might not allow us to stay out late, or even go out at all, the next weekend. How strictly you enforce curfew is up to you, but it seems that ruling with an iron fist will get the best results.

Four: ruling with an iron fist. This isn't what it seems. Yes, you should be tough on curfew, but when I say tough, I mean tough on communication. Suppose we're running late and we text you, "Hey, I'm going to be around 10–15 minutes late, it was tough finding a ride home!" There should be no consequences or problems, and the response should be, "OK got it!" However, if we show up late with no legitimate excuse, then yes, you should get mad and confront us about it. When it comes to nights when you know we're out late, then *please* accept calls from unknown phones, because chances are our phone either died or isn't working and we're trying to call you on someone else's phone. I find it extremely annoying when I repeatedly try to call my parents but they refuse to answer because they don't recognize the number on caller ID.

It seems that curfew is more of a communication problem than a time problem; therefore, it is absolutely essential to reiterate to your kids that they must text or call whenever they have a problem, check in when they're supposed to, and check in when they are running late. If you can create a pattern and enforce a fair and reasonable curfew, then hopefully this topic won't be as disputed in your family as it is in mine.

Paralleling government laws, curfew should get later as your teen gets older. Being eighteen and having an eleven o'clock curfew is completely unreasonable. Oh yeah, one last thing: Teens are always going to fight for a later curfew. So if we're good, then give us a later curfew; and if we're bad, well, you know what to do.

Social Networking

Social networks, such as MySpace and Facebook, are one of the best ways for teens to maintain stable relationships with faraway friends and family and also stay in tune with current events. I first got a Facebook account in eighth grade and scarcely used it. When I got older and moved away from Ohio, I started using my account frequently to stay in touch with old friends and meet new ones in California. I highly praise social networks for helping people maintain and build friendships. Then again, these websites are not always safe, and misuse of an account can cause extreme consequences. This chapter will cover most, if not all, of the situations that may arise from your teen joining a social network.

One: set the right age to create an account. Most kids get social network accounts right when they turn thirteen years old. This may seem early, but it is perfectly fine as long as the majority of their friends have accounts too. Make sure your kids know that social networks are useful only if their friends have accounts on the same website, otherwise they'll be posting photos and status updates for no one but strangers to see (depending on account security preferences), completely defeating the purpose of joining a network and interacting with friends. As long as your kids' friends are registered on a site, or plan to register soon, then it's fine for your kids to join the network.

Two: becoming friends on networks. Parents should let their kids create accounts on social networks, but if you are worried about what your kids might do on them, simply friend them or subscribe to their webpage to find out what they do (but please avoid stalking them—that gets annoying). However, if your kids don't allow you to become friends or subscribe to them, it isn't necessarily a bad thing. It just means you should ground them for five weeks (*just* kidding). If this problem occurs, talk to your kids or keep sending requests until they do accept. You could ask them what they have to hide that's so bad and inform them that by posting photos of drinking or anything illegal, they can ruin job and college opportunities. If these tactics don't work, then it's better to let them be and not try to friend them. After all, if what your teenager posts is really bad (and that means like crazy stupid things), you will for sure hear about it from other parents. That's how some of my friends get grounded occasionally.

Three: posting photos. Make sure your kids know that any photos of them consuming illegal beverages or doing anything else illegal can stay on the Internet forever as soon as they click the upload button. It is very important to keep these kinds of photos offline, or simply never take the photos at all. If your kids' friends are the ones uploading photos like this, your kids can easily untag themselves and ask the friends to remove the photos. After all, colleges, family, parents, and future employers can see any of these photos, ultimately creating a bad impression.

Four: relationship status. Your kids' relationship status isn't a very big deal. Don't be surprised if it says married, engaged, in a relationship, or dating, because a lot of teens (mostly girls) do this with their best friends. For example, you might see "Susie is engaged to Laura." This should not be taken seriously. It is mostly just best friends showing their appreciation of each other. However, if your teen's relationship status says in a relationship with someone of the opposite sex, then it most likely is true. In the end, though, relationship statuses are minor problems and should not be stressed over.

Five: appropriate status updates. A status is a message that all your friends can see; for example, "I'm so excited for Friday!" Statuses are the most annoying of all the problems on social networking sites. Nothing is more stupid then posting a status that admits to doing illegal things, attacks a group or individual, or expresses something vulgar. About half of all international news reports about the negative effects of social networks involve status updates. For example, some teens say that they hate their teachers, that they love to drink or smoke, or that they want to hurt an individual or group. This almost *always* gets kids in trouble with parents, school, or the law (especially when it involves threats).

Definitely tell your kids to watch their status updates and refrain from posting their problems to their webpage.

Remember, it is definitely okay for your kids to have social networking accounts, as long as they are responsible and mature while using them.

Personal Expression

One of the most important things in middle school is blending in with those around you. However, come high school, your teenager may assume an entirely different mentality. Here's how to embrace this change.

Whether it's baggy jeans, tight jeans, low jeans, high jeans, ripped jeans, faded jeans, black jeans, or blue jeans, teenagers express themselves through clothing. But in order to best understand this, we need to go back to chapter 5 and remember the phrase *Don't judge a book by its cover*. This super-clichéd line tells the truth for all teenagers. Just because some teens dye their hair and spike it in crazy ways or rock super preppy clothes and a popped collar, it doesn't necessarily mean those kids fit the role.

Typically, adults label teens with spiked hair and black clothing as rebellious. That's only because all the teenage help hotlines and parenting books have branded these teens as rebels of society.

I know a lot of kids who dress or act like this, and they have great relationships with their parents and friends. I also know teens who dress like model students and have bad relationships with their parents and assume less-than-healthy habits. Truly, clothing is simply something we wear on our back. It may cause us to stand out, or it may cause us to blend in with society and friends, but that's what all teenagers want. We want our clothes to get us individual attention from others, but at the same time we want acceptance in our group of friends and our family.

Accept and compliment the way your teen looks, and never assume something negative just because of their personal expression.

Conclusion
(this is where I leave you)

Ok, I've done my best to help you understand how to get along with your teen. And, remember, I'm just one teen with one perspective. But if any of my tips or thoughts have helped you have a better relationship with your kid, this time I've spent writing this book will be worthwhile. I'd love to hear from you if I've helped or if you have other questions. Please visit my facebook page Teens Happen and follow me on twitter @TeensHappen.

And remember, in spite of parents, teens turn out ok.

About the Author

Photo by Dana Fineman

Shea Rouda is one of four children and was born in Columbus, Ohio. In early high school he developed an interest in writing. After moving to Malibu, California, in 2009, he pursued this hobby more seriously and wrote his first book, *Teens Happen*.

CPSIA information can be obtained at www.ICGtesting.com
Printed in the USA
BVOW011822191011

274076BV00001B/62/P